MW00915261

RICH WITCH

POWERFUL SPELLS, RITUALS & HABITS TO SKYROCKET YOUR PROSPERITY

By: Zelda Barrons

Discount on Psychic Readings, Aura Readings and Tarot Readings for my Readers

I have TONS of book bonuses for you including my free Psychic Masterclass, a discount code for a personal reading with me, access to a members only fb group and more.

Register for your free book bonuses here: https://tinyurl.com/zeldamailgifts

Praise for Zelda Barrons' work:

"Zelda's readings are by far the most spiritual and worthy of attention. Not only providing a decisive prediction for future, but she also focuses on life lessons and why I am in this situation now. Her guidance is totally non-judgmental and very gentle."

"I think I just met my new best friend.... Zelda was so on point that it was scary. I also appreciate that she told me what the cards said and not what I wanted to hear. Thank you again!"

"Thank you for answering my follow up questions so effectively. They may seem rather obvious and routine, but those are the thoughts that we need to squash, and you have been so helpful in doing that. Thank you so much for your guidance!"

"All I can say is WOW! She was so accurate, I had goosebumps. Zelda's reading encompassed what was coming up and she also talked about what I was doing now. I am so excited that I'm on the right track."

"Absolutely amazing! So much information, wow! She's your girl for insight!!"

"I'm truly satisfied with Zelda's reading. She is truly in tune with the situation without any judgement and she gave me a guidance that was very helpful. She continued her reading in the comment section to thoroughly explain and answer to my questions. Thank you so much!!!"

"Wow!! The reading was so in depth and concise, and she explained all other cards and gave me her insights in the comment section. I was deeply moved. Zelda is a great spiritual teacher to show my best path and empowered me to move forward!! Thank you so much!!"

"What a beautiful soul!! This reading was excellent and very accurate and also very empowering!! I loved the way advice was given to personally empower!!! Would highly recommend."

"Very detailed and amazing. I truly appreciate the continued follow up in the comments. Thank you is not enough."

"Zelda Barrons is the best! She saw my situation clearly and eased my troubled heart. Her insight is phenomenal. I'll definitely be back and I highly recommend her to everyone."

"Hmmmmm what to say about Zelda? To be honest, there are no words that can describe her...she is exceptional and one of the best honest readers I have ever had the pleasure to read for me!!!!! Thank you so much...."

"Excellent reading and insight, with a caring spirit! The additional clarification was wonderful and appreciated. Actions I've started to already take were also confirmed. Thank you so much!"

"Really great reading. Loved the cards and delivery style, very different but so informative and detailed. Zelda is a beautiful compassionate spirit. Most definitely recommend."

"Spot on and very insightful! My reading by Zelda was so helpful and absolutely dead on. She was extremely detailed and insightful when interpreting the cards for my situation. I will definitely use her again when I need quick clarity in my life and business."

This book is dedicated to you

CONTENTS

A LOVE LETTER TO MY READERS

Dear friends,

Thank you so much for reading this book. Together we are raising the consciousness of the whole planet! After all, the more money you have, the more people and animals you can help. You can do so many good things for the world with money.

While this isn't the first money spell book out there, it is the first book to combine spellwork with universal laws and Psychology so that your results are backed by science. This is also the only spell book that will tell you exactly how and why each spell works.

You can be whatever kind of rich witch you desire. You get to decide whether you live off the grid on a farm (like me soon) or in a fancy high rise in the city, or anywhere else for that matter. As you read this book, take what resonates with you and leave the rest. You have the power. You get to decide.

Whether you're a young teen dabbling in spells for the first time or an adult who wants to tip the wealth odds in your favor, this book is for you.

I'm an open minded person. So these spells are for you no matter what your religion, race or gender. And while I may refer to you as "gorgeous" or "she", this book is for anyone who wants to read it regardless of their gender or orientation. As RuPaul says, "We're all born naked and the rest is just drag." Can I get an Amen?

I share a ton of my own personal stories in this book. I'm definitely not perfect, but I've come a long way. That's why I know abundance is possible for you too. Because I went to the school of hard knocks and learned all this the hard way. The good news is you don't have to because you can learn from me and my mentors.

Think of this book as a nourishing potion...it's a delightful combination of all the wonderful things, techniques and ideas I've had the pleasure of learning over the last few decades. And while some of the ideas may not be brand new, I've put my own unique spin on them to explain them in a way that only I can, so that it all makes sense for you.

This book is my gift to you and the world. May it help you skyrocket your abundance and your happiness. In order to receive this gift fully, read this book with an open mind and an open heart. You totally deserve it!

Without further ado, let's get started!

Love, Glitter & truckloads of joy,

Zelda

PS. **Register for your free book bonuses here: https://tinyurl.com/zeldamailgifts**
. Do it ASAP before you forget. You are worth it! Bonuses include my free Psychic Masterclass, a discount

code for a personal reading with me, access to a members only fb group and more.

Register for your free book bonuses here: https://tinyurl.com/zeldamailgifts

INTRODUCTION

Your words are so incredibly powerful. YOU are so incredibly powerful. Your mindset is your most powerful asset. Your mindset, will power and intention are the only key ingredients you truly need in order to shift your reality. So you'll notice that most of these spells and rituals require very few ingredients. If you're missing one of two of the ingredients, the spells will still work if you believe they will and if you are coming from the right mindset. That said, using special ingredients and tools with spells is so incredibly fun! The tools also help you form a stronger connection with the spell.

Before you dive in and create a wildly prosperous life with your new bestie (ahem, this book) by your side, I want to share with you how and why these spells work.

Your subconscious mind is responsible for making your heartbeat and all the other automatic actions that you don't have to think about. Your Subconscious Mind is ALWAYS working behind the scenes without any effort from you. It's always listening too! On the other hand, your conscious mind is the often judgy mind that says, "this will never work." So these spells offer a shortcut that bypass the conscious mind and go right to the subconscious, where the real magic happens.

What is a spell? When you powerfully focus your energy and intentions to bring about a specific result, that is a spell. Spells help to focus and flow your energy toward what it is you desire.

You will notice that some spells suggest a specific moonphase to get the best results. You can look up what phase the moon is in by googling "Moon Phases 2019" or whatever year it is right now.

Traditionally, waxing moon (waxing moon means the moon is getting bigger) time is best for abundance spells, while waning moon (means the moon is getting smaller) is best when you want to get rid of something.

The Law of Abundance states, "People become wealthy because they decide to become wealthy."

Make the decision now. You get to decide. If you say, "this doesn't work." That is your decision too.

"We receive what we believe."

In Amy Steinberg's Law of Abundance article, she says, "Our job is to be in alignment with this Truth. There is always enough. Always. And from this place of deep gratitude and awareness, we are changing the world."

Belief and trust are essential. It's important that you believe you are going to get what you set out to create with these spells and rituals. Why? Because if you are full of skepticism, doubt, mistrust, fear and other lower energy emotions, you will be a MATCH to that yucky energy, not to the super fun and high-vibration energy of abundance.

Psychology has proven that the Placebo Effect is indeed real and POWERFUL. The Placebo effect means that patients can be cured by their belief alone. I don't know about you, but if I'm a rich witch and I made it happen *only* because of my belief, I'd still be pretty happy with that.

"Whether you believe you are rich or not, you're right."

Science proves time and time again that our perceptions shape and create our reality.

"When you become the image of your own imagination, it's the most powerful thing you could ever do." - RuPaul

How to Increase a Spell's Power: Flow VS. Hustle

"Destroy the idea that you have to be constantly working or grinding in order to be successful. Embrace the essential concept that rest, recovery, reflection are essential parts of the progress toward a successful and happy life." - Zach Galifianakis

One of my clients is a workaholic. It's normal for her to spend 14 hours on the computer, then stay up late to watch a show (or 10) to decompress. You'd think with the amount of time she spends working, that she would be wealthy, right? Unfortunately, you'd be wrong. Lucy does mostly "busy work" that doesn't produce much income or results. She's stuck in the old masculine business model that is not only outdated, but it's unhealthy too.

"Everyday I'm hustlin," - Your Subconscious Mind

Hustling is for your subconscious mind, not for rich witches. In America, it's unfortunately seen as virtuous to skip sleep and work constantly so that you can do more, more, more and buy more and more and more. This message is not healthy or balanced. Especially for women, because our energy levels fluctuate with our cycles.

Rich witches understand the importance of rest and tranquility. Rest isn't something nice to have like a luxury. Rest is essential. Afterall, life is all about balance. If you are devoting too much energy and effort to any

ONE thing in your life, you'll be off balance. And if you allow yourself to be too "busy" all the time, you will miss subtle cues from your intuition. You may feel stressed out. You may "hustle" yourself right into ill health or adrenal fatigue. Health is wealth!

In order to receive anything, you need to be in a receptive state. "Hustling" is the opposite of receptivity. Receptivity is allowing, flowing, and not trying to force the outcome.

While doing these spells will fill you with positivity and send a flood of inspired ideas your way (straight outta your intuition), you won't be required to work 24/7 or hustle to increase your wealth. But you will have to take inspired action on any ideas that excite you after you cast these spells. Got it?

The money can come from a variety of places. You might receive a check in the mail, find money in the street, or receive money in other ways. The key is to be open to the millions of possibilities and ways that money can come. If you find a penny in the street, pick it up! This is a sign that more is on the way.

You might be offered overtime if you have a job. You may get a raise or a promotion. You may be inspired to ASK for a raise. You might start looking for a new job or change careers. You may decide to start a side business.

If you're in business for yourself, you might get a new client (or 10)! You may receive a flood of ideas for new services or products to create. This book in your hand is the result of one of my inspired ideas.

Science has proven that everything is energy. And according to the law of correspondence (as above, so below), like energy attracts like energy. So in order for spells to have a lot of power, **you** have to have a lot of power/energy.

But how? You become powerful when you RAISE your energy and get in a high-vibrational state...Abraham Hicks calls this the Vortex. Mihaly Csikszentmihalyi calls this FLOW. Athletes call it the ZONE. Whatever you call it, you have to FEEL good when you are casting these spells if you want mind blowing results!

High energy states and emotions such as joy, love, appreciation and excitement are what you are aiming for. Because you can't create amazing abundance unless if you are already feeling that way. You can't create wealth from a place a lack.

Another potent way to increase each spell's power is to visualize the end result as if it was already in your life. How will you feel? What actions will you take? See yourself taking those actions and allow yourself to feel those emotions right now. Even top athletes use visualization to create incredible results.

Everything is created in the mind first. This book you're reading was once an idea in my brain. Every building you see, was once just an idea. Every new dish you try at a restaurant was also once just an idea.

A third way to skyrocket each spell's power, is to ask yourself, "what is the goal behind the goal?" In order words, what would having more money in your life mean for you? How can you give yourself more of that quality now?

For example, money means freedom to me. So in order for my spells to work ultra fast, I must give myself freedom **now**. This could mean taking a walk outside or traveling to a new location. It could mean taking the day off or allowing myself to sleep late. It might mean ripping up my to-do list. When I feel free, I'm ultra powerful.

Money might mean security for you. How can you give yourself more security NOW, even without truckloads of cash? You might start by creating a stash of emergency food. Or by showing yourself that you are worth taking care of. Make yourself a priority. Money won't buy you security if you are catering to everyone else's whims first.

For best results: before you do one of these spells and rituals, get in the mindset of joy, appreciation, love, excitement, or another POSITIVE emotion. Heck, watch a kitten or puppy video on youtube before you get started if you have to. Even Tony Robbins jumps on a trampoline before his live events to get his energy up. The result? His audience is *spellbound*.

You will notice that after each spell, I instruct you to be on the lookout for signs and to actually EXPECT the moolah to show up. This is not about 'positive thinking' rah-rah hogwash or faking it til you make it. It's more like, "don't dream it, BE it." When you believe and behave like a rich witch NOW, the universe will send you opportunities that are a match to that energy.

What would a rich witch do? After each spell, it's imperative that you ACT how you would act if you had the money in your hot little hands. I'm not asking you to quit your sheisty job or spend outrageous sums of money you don't have, but to ask yourself what would you do today if you knew you could create the money easily at will? And then, do it! You might be compelled to visit a new part of town. You might feel the urge to start a new hobby. Follow your intuition!

For example, a client said to me said that if she were rich, she'd spend more time creating art just for fun. But in her current life, she never made the time for it.

I replied, "but you can create art in your spare time now, why wait?"

So Julia took my advice. And those cat doodles she made time for? They became a lucrative side business!

Do yourself a favor and start with the first spell listed, which is called Clearing the Obstacles.

Warning: Please be sure to follow basic safety precautions. Never leave a lit candle unattended. I typically set a reminder on my phone to blow out the candle. Be sure not to reach over a lit candle or open flame with flowing clothing or long hair. I am speaking from experience, singed hair and all.

When you burn sage, open a window for ventilation and be sure to snuff it out with sand or water so it doesn't reignite without you knowing.

Here we go!

FAQS

I decided to put these frequently asked questions in the beginning of this book for a good reason. Because you will get plenty of AHA moments and a chance to "troubleshoot" your spells from these frequently asked questions before you begin to cast the spells.

Q: How come you didn't include a spell for winning the lottery?

I will explain exactly why in a moment. First let me tell you a little story about a friend of mine.

Liz had her heart set on winning the lottery. She bought piles of tickets every week and never really won anything. So I asked Liz why she wanted to win. She admitted that the lottery was the "only way" that she could have that amount of money.

Liz's answer to my question explained her mindset. In reality, there are over a million ways that a million dollars could show up for you, *but she only saw one way*: the lottery. So Liz was not a match to abundance. Her mindset was one of scarcity. And that's why she never won anything. Because if you're doing something from a place of lack (whether that's buying a lottery ticket or casting a spell), you can only create more lack.

Even the Bible basically says that "more will be given to those that have"....and the "more" they are speaking of is FAITH.

My friend Liz seemed to have no faith in herself and saw the lottery as her "rescue".

When I asked Liz what she wanted the money for (and this is a biggie), instead of telling me about all the great stuff she wanted to do with the money, she said she wanted to use it as a way to avoid working and avoid creating something new. Bingo. Whenever you're running away from something, you cannot create abundance from that space.

Furthermore, Liz revealed a belief she held for decades: That charging for her services was wrong. And that she felt like a "good person" for not charging. This put Liz in a terrible predicament. She could either be a "good poor person" or a "terrible rich person."

So I asked Liz if she thought that buying food or paying rent or taking care of her family was somehow wrong. And of course she laughed and said, "No, everybody needs to eat. In this country, you need to go to the grocery store to buy food. And for that you need money."

So I asked Liz a clarifying question that opened her eyes: "Would you rather be poor and "honorable" or start charging for your services and be able to feed your family?"

Suddenly Liz saw the connection. She had a deep-seated belief that rich people are evil or wrong.

"They can't ALL be bad," I replied.

So I asked Liz to prove herself wrong by looking up examples of wealthy people who are generous and donate to charity and other causes they believe in.

For example, J.K. Rowling gave so much to charity that she went from a billionaire to a millionaire. Bill Gates has given away over 27 billion dollars so far!

I'm not a millionaire (yet) but I regularly donate to animal charities and other causes I believe in.

If you can relate to this story or have a money belief you want to shift, start looking for EVIDENCE and prove yourself wrong. You and your bank account can thank me later.

Q. What about the Law of Attraction? Can I do that too?

I'm all about harnessing universal laws to create massive results in your life. The issue with the law of attraction is that is teaches you to "attract" something that you are missing. Why is that a problem? Because everything you could ever want, already exists.

A better way to get what you to desire is NOT to wish for or hope for it. It's to DECIDE you will have it. Accept it as a fact. That's how magic works.

The universe mirrors your beliefs and feelings back to you...therefore if you're feeling a lack of money in your life, there's another area in your life that is feeling a lack and needs your attention.

One of my clients told me she was "doing the law of attraction" on a certain guy she likes, but the more she tried, the more he ignored her and ghosted her. This is because people have free will, and when you try to control the outcome, you close off the flow. She was feeling a lack of worth and wanted this guy's attention in order to feel worthy. And because she was putting out a ton of "needy" lack energy, that's what she was getting back. And whatever you "need", you push away. This is the opposite of being receptive.

Remember Elmira from Tiny Tunes who practically squeezed the animals she loved to death? She is the best example of NEEDY energy. Animals always tried to run away from her. Similarly, needy energy repels money, opportunities and people.

Q. How many spells can I do? Can I do them all? Can I try them all in one day?

I don't recommend trying all of these spells in one day. This is because the energy of desperation or neediness repels money. Why? Because lower vibrations repel all the goodies you desire. There's no need to cast all of these spells in one day. One spell is really all you need.

What I recommend doing is picking a few spells that resonate with you and trying them out over the course of a month or two. Give them time to work their magic. Eventually you can do all of the spells in the book, but it will take much longer than a day.

Q. I tried one of the spells. It's been 1 whole day and I haven't seen any results. Why not?

18

The most important key to successful spell work happens BEFORE you cast the spells.

Did you get excited first? Did you visualize about what you would do with the money? Are you giving all that wonderful money a place to go? Did you allow yourself to feel how you would feel when you receive it? Were you specific about what you wanted to receive the money for? Did you imagine yourself spending it in a way that fills you with joy? Did you truly believe you would receive it?

If you said no to any of these questions, you are blocking your spell from working. This is good because it means YOU have the power to change that.

When you affirm that you haven't seen results (after only a day), you are pushing away everything that you were on your way to aligning with.

Give your spells two to three weeks and look for evidence the entire time. Be consistent with gratitude and be open to seeing signs. The more grateful and happy you are, the more money you will align with.

Everything comes at the right time. It is possible that a spell may work for you later (rather than now) because there may be something you need to learn first. Trust the timing of the universe.

Q.You mention looking for signs or evidence that the spells are working. What kind of signs?

Finding money in the street (even a penny) is evidence that you are aligning with money. Celebrate when you find coins!

Here are some other signs you may experience. You may:
- Receive an unexpected gift, card or something else of value
- Find coins in the street, in your pockets, or in the dryer
- Hear about opportunities you were wondering about
- Come across books, movies and songs that have messages for you
- Be invited on a trip or fun outing
- Receive more compliments than usual
- Experience meaningful coincidences and synchronicities

Want even more signs? Write them down in order to increase them!

Q. I don't consider myself a witch. Can I still try these spells?

I'll let you in a little secret. I've been studying universal laws and metaphysics decades before before witchcraft became trendy. And I don't even call myself a witch. Labels are for products, not people. You can try any of these spells you like. No label required.

PART 1: RICH WITCH SPELLS

CLEARING THE OBSTACLES TO PROSPERITY SPELL

"True wealth is having the knowledge to maneuver and navigate the mental obstacles that inhibit your ability to soar." RuPaul

Money is called currency because it is meant to flow, like water. If your bathroom sink is clogged with hair and other sludge, then the water can't flow because there are obstacles in the way. Similarly, if you have obstacles in the way of money, it won't flow to you.

What obstacles? Denise Duffield Thomas and other money mindset experts call these obstacles "money blocks" because they block money from showing up in your life.

Regardless of what you call them, most obstacles to riches are mental or emotional ones. For example, a belief that you don't deserve money. Or a false belief that money is bad. Or a false belief that rich people are bad. Obstacles can show up as self sabotage, such as blowing all of your cash immediately or giving it all away for example. You might want to raise your prices (if you sell a service or product) but be too afraid to change your prices. Or like one of my friends, you might be afraid to charge anything at all.

In order to create money, you must believe that you deserve money and that having money is actually a good thing.

Regardless of what your obstacles are, this spell will help to clear the path for more money to show up in your life. Do this spell as often as once a day if you need to.

Ingredients: one white candle, a white sheet of paper, a red pen, salt

Moonphase: waning, which means there is less light and the moon is getting smaller. This happens directly after a full moon to the time of the new moon.

STEP ONE: GRAB YOUR RED PEN AND SHEET OF PAPER. START WRITING ANY OBSTACLES TO WEALTH THAT COME TO MIND. DON'T BE AFRAID TO WRITE DOWN THE NEGATIVE. THE POINT OF THIS SPELL IS TO CLEAR

AND GET RID OF ALL THIS CRUD THAT'S IN THE WAY OF THE WEALTH THAT IS RIGHTFULLY YOURS.

You may use as many sheets of paper as you need to write down your obstacles.

STEP TWO:
SPRINKLE A PINCH
OF SALT ON THE
SHEET OF PAPER.
IMAGINE THE
OBSTACLES
SHRINKING TO THE
SIZE OF A GRAIN OF
SALT. IMAGINE THE
SALT SUCKING THE
POWER OUT OF THE
OBSTACLES LIKE A
VACUUM.

STEP THREE: LIGHT THE WHITE CANDLE

STEP FOUR: SPRINKLE A BIT OF SALT FROM THE PAPER ONTO TO CANDLE

Say this out loud:

"This salt dissolves the obstacles that once bound me
This flame eats the salt and now I'm free
By the power of three, so mote it be
For the good of all involved, it is done"

Step five: Blow out the candle, tear up the paper(s), and go do something fun.

If you have extra stubborn obstacles, EFT (Emotional Freedom Technique) can work wonders to help you clear them. Just go on Youtube and search for Brad Yates EFT or Kim Eibrink Jansen EFT. You can do EFT every day. EFT is simple but amazingly effective on a variety of issues.

This clearing spell can be done as often as three times a week. Stubborn beliefs didn't form overnight, and they won't always go away overnight either.

Why this works: This spell works because when you write down the beliefs you want to clear, you are clearing your mind and making room for focused intentions, which means more powerful spells. Salt is used to clear, cleanse, and banish that which does not serve you. The fire transmutes the salt and carries your intentions into the universe.

Can't think of any obstacles? Go back to your childhood and think of a time when you overheard someone say, "money doesn't grow on trees" or other guilt-inducing phrases about money. Did someone try to make you feel "greedy" for wanting a second slice of cake? Get it all out on the paper. Are you afraid to ask for money that people owe you because you don't want to be "mean"? Has anyone ever stolen from you, so now you're afraid to have nice things because you believe someone will just take it anyway? Write it down.

For example, my parents always forced me to share with my little sister. I had to share my Halloween candy, my clothes, my room and pretty much anything else she wanted. As I got older, I was so afraid that as soon as I got rich, mooches would come crawling out of the woodwork with their hands out for me to "share" with them. This was a huge obstacle for me. As soon as I cleared it, I replaced it with the knowledge that as an adult, I don't have to share with anyone unless if I want to. After the path was cleared, the the money flowed in like gangbusters!

MORNING TEA SPELL AKA PROSPERI-TEA

"Where there's tea there's hope."-Sir Arthur Pinero

Do this simple, yet powerful spell every day if you wish.

Ingredients: Your favorite morning beverage of choice, a spoon

Moonphase: any

STEP ONE: PREPARE YOUR BEVERAGE OR TEA

STEP TWO: ALLOW YOURSELF TO GET EXCITED OR HAPPY. PRO TIP: YOU MAY HAVE TO WATCH KITTENS ON YOUTUBE OR LOOK AT FUNNY MEMES UNTIL YOU ARE LAUGHING SO HARD THAT TEARS ROLL DOWN YOUR CHEEKS.

STEP THREE: STIR YOUR DRINK CLOCKWISE THREE TIMES AS YOU JOYFULLY CHANT:

"Three by three, three by three,

everything I give comes back to me

For the good of all, So mote it be. Thank you, thank you, thank you."

STEP THREE: DRINK YOUR TEA/BEVERAGE

Step four: Do a good deed today. Choose from one of the following.

- Give someone a sincere compliment
- Open the door for a stranger
- Pay for a stranger's coffee
- Visit animals at a shelter
- Leave a dollar or a quarter on the ground for some lucky kid to find
- Donate something to Goodwill or another thrift shop

One of my clients tried this with fantastic results. Alice was thrilled to tell me she sold several new products (worth thousands of dollars each) after doing this morning tea spell for 3 days.

Why this spell works: The power of water and intention has been documented and studied extensively by Dr. Masaru Emoto. His book The Hidden Messages In Water was a NY Times Bestseller. We can use this power for better or for worse.

For over two decades, Dr. Masaru Emoto has successfully documented the molecular changes in water to show the effects that our words, thoughts, and intentions have on the water crystals.

For example, water from clear mountain springs had beautifully formed crystals that were pleasant to look at, while polluted water formed crystals that were deformed and misshapen.

MONEY-TRIPLING SPELL

"Three is the magic number."- Schoolhouse Rock

This is a simple spell that you can use to triple the amount of paper money that you have.

Ingredients: a mirror, a white envelope, a purple or green or gold pen, paper money in any denomination (example, five $20 bills). The larger the denomination, the more you will receive. You can use more than one note/dollar bill if you desire.

Moon Phase: Waxing, which means the moon is growing bigger and brighter.

Step one: Close your eyes and imagine your wallet stuffed with triple the amount of money you currently have. Your subconscious mind doesn't know if the images you see are real or imagined, so take your time and really see all the details in the mind. Imagine what this money will smell like. Imagine how it feels to have this amount in your wallet. Imagine joyfully spending this money on an experience that delights you. Imagine knowing that there is plenty more where that came from.

Step two: Open your eyes. Make sure the dollar bills are facing up and all facing the same way. Place them neatly in the envelope. Seal the envelope.

Step three: Grab your pen and write what you intend to buy with this money on the envelope followed by the word, "thank you". But write it in the past tense.

For example: "I used the extra money to buy groceries. Thank you."

You need to write in the past tense, as if you already received it.

STEP FOUR: PLACE THE ENVELOPE ON THE MIRROR.

Step five: Close your eyes and imagine the envelope getting bigger and fatter, practically overflowing with money. Imagine how heavy this envelope feels in your hands now that there is three times as much money inside. Imagine yourself spending the money on what you wrote about on the envelope. See the cashier at the store. Or see the check going to the mortgage company. Bite into that apple in your mind.

Step five: Say this, "Powers that be, triple this sum, I thank you kindly for all that comes.

By the power of three, so mote it be. For the good of all involved, it is done."

Do this spell once a day for 3 days straight. Keep the envelope on the mirror when you are not using it to cast the spell.

The extra money won't just appear in the envelope, but it will show up in your life within 21 days via synchronicity and other meaningful "coincidences" and opportunities. Remember to expect it. Follow any intuitive hunches you get. Your intuition will be extra chatty with you. It's up to you to follow it.

After you've received the money, open the envelope and either spend or deposit the cash.

If you want to cast this spell again in the near future, you must use a new set of bills and a fresh envelope.

Why this spell works: Giving your money a place to flow to is powerful. But the icing on the cake is the writing. This is why you write what you intend to use the money for. Writing activates your brain's reticular activating system (RAS), which is the brain's filter. Writing will call your attention to anything that pertains to what you wrote down...in this case, increasing your wealth.

The RAS is the gatekeeper of information to your conscious mind. So when you write things down, your neural pathways are strengthened and your brain will know to be on the lookout for opportunities. When you write out your goals and visualise, you program your RAS to see new patterns. You literally train your brain to see opportunities.

I told one of my friends about this spell. She called me from the mall a few hours later. After she casted the spell, she had decided to go for a walk at the mall. She found a pile of cash at the mall while walking around.

MONEY JAR SPELL

"Money is just candy that hasn't been born yet." -
Tina Belcher, Bob's Burgers

This spell is meant to work continuously. Your going to make your jar once and leave it out where you can see it everyday. Every time you need a financial boost, just shake the jar three times (with feeling!) and recite the chant.

Ingredients: a clear jar with a lid, 33 coins, 3 bay leaves, 3 cinnamon sticks, a small green or red candle, a sheet of paper, a green pen

Moonphase: waxing (growing bigger, like your wallet)

Optional Ingredients: 3 pretty rocks or seashells that you find outside in nature, 3 citrine crystals, 3 amethyst crystals

Step one: light your candle. Then add all of your items to your jar

Step two: shake the jar 3 times while allowing yourself to get excited about all the money on the way. You can jump up and down with the jar if you wish. Don't half-ass it or you will get half-assed results.

STEP THREE: CHANT THE FOLLOWING:

"prosperity, prosperity,

This jar brings money and luck to me

For the good of all, so mote it be."

Optional Step four: Place the jar in the sun for 3 hours to energize the ingredients

Mandatory Step four: write 3 things you are grateful for and stick it in your jar

For example: I'm grateful for my bed, my health, my clothes, etc. If you have trouble feeling grateful for your living situation, go camping for the weekend. Zelda's orders! Do it. You will definitely appreciate having running water and electricity and a real bed to sleep in when you get home! � �

Final Step: Leave the jar on a shelf where you can see it everyday

I have several of these fun jars around my house. Not only do they attract compliments from visitors, but they work. My friend Cheryl created a spell jar for the purpose of going on a trip to Greece. She sent me a postcard from Greece a few months ago.

Why this works? Seeing this jar everyday acts as a visual anchor and reminder that your jar is magnetizing money into your life. Shaking the jar amplifies and directs the energy to where it needs to go. Showing yourself that you already have abundance creates even more.

Fun Variation: Place a jar of colorful gumballs, marbles or seashells (you decide) next to the money jar to delight your inner child.

MONEY MAGNET SPELL

"Real generosity is doing something nice for someone who will never find out."- Frank A. Clark

Ingredients: 8 coins. Either quarters, nickels, dimes or pennies will do. The more the coin is worth, the better this spell works.You'll need 8 total of the same kind of coin.

Moonphase: any

Step one: With the 8 coins in your pocket, go to a public place. The ideal place is somewhere you can't be seen putting the coins down, but where you know someone will see them later.

Step two: Hold the coins in your left hand and project happiness into them for 60 seconds. Once again, this is where your imagination and cute animal videos comes in handy. You can also remember a happy memory or event from your life. Really FEEL it!

Step three: Place the charged coins down in the shape of a smiley face, using one coin for each eye, and the rest of the coins for a mouth.

STEP FOUR: SAY THIS SPELL (OR JUST THINK IT IN YOUR HEAD IF PEOPLE ARE AROUND):

"Coins of 8, I set you free

I trust you'll come right back to me

With many more you'll bring along

Giving joy where you belong

By the power of 3, so mote it be

For the good of all involved, it is done."

I've had amazing results placing the coins on a playground, at a park, and in parking lots.

Resist the temptation to stick around and spy on people who pick up the coins. You can do this spell three times a week if you wish.

Why this works: When you give freely, you are showing the universe that you know there is plenty available. If you act stingy, the universe will be stingy with you! So when you do this spell, you are showing that you trust the money to come back to you in other ways. The people who find the coins will have their days "made" brighter, so you are helping to create a positive ripple of joy. The universe will reward you. Expect it.

A friend of mine tried this spell and shared her fun idea and results with me. Kelley decided to leave dollars on the windshields of cars outside of the dollar store. Within a few days, she received a call from someone who offered to pay her to teach a class she was thinking of teaching.

UNEXPECTED GIFTS MONEY SPELL

"Give it to me, I'm worth it."- Fifth Harmony

This spell will help you recognize (and therefore increase) all that the universe is giving to you. When you let other people give to you, you are giving them the joy of giving! Despite what society says about it, receiving isn't selfish at all.

Feminine energy is receptive. All beings have feminine and masculine energies, regardless of their gender. Sometimes these energies get thrown out of balance. So if you want to increase the amount of money, gifts, and everything else that you receive, you have to amp up your receptivity or ability to receive.

Ingredients: a large bowl, 33 coins of any type, a pink candle, a notebook, pink marker

Optional: Add 3 pieces each of rose quartz and citrine to the bowl

Moonphase: waxing

Prior to doing this spell, place the 33 coins in a clear glass jar outside in the moonlight to charge overnight. The moon represents feminine energy.

Step one: Place the ingredients in the bowl. Allow yourself to get happy and excited.

STEP TWO: LIGHT THE CANDLE

STEP THREE: SAY THE FOLLOWING:

"As above and so below

I am like this large bowl

Filled to the brim

and lightning swift

Thank you for the future gifts

What's here now I recognize

Thank you for the sweet surprise"

Step four: Blow the candle out. Alwayskeep the bowl out where you can see it so this spell works constantly. When you get spare change, place the change in the bowl and say thank you.

Asyou go about your daily life, notice how you react when people give you compliments, hold the door for you or try to buy you lunch. If you accept these gifts with an open heart, you will receive more. But if you feel guilty or say, "no thanks" when you receive, you are telling the universe to send these gifts and money to other people! (I learned this from Maru Iabichela, the wonderful creator of Infinite Receiving.)

If you feel uncomfortable accepting gifts and compliments, it's time for you to do the Clearing the Obstacles spell again.

Step five: As you receive unexpected compliments, gifts, money and more, write it in your notebook. Place the notebook next to your bowl.

Step six: What gifts in your life are you ignoring? Wear your favorite jewelry and your favorite clothes. As you GIVE to yourself, the universe will give back to you.

My friend Dee is a very type-A kind of gal. But she was drawn to this spell for some reason. She texted to tell me that she received 4 new marketing clients within a week of casting this spell.

Why this spell works: The moon represents feminine energy. You are charging the coins with feminine energy so that you can receive more in your life. We're using a bowl which also represents feminine energy. As you fill the bowl in this spell, your intentions flow out to the universe and give your subconscious mind a job to do in watching out for ways you can create it. As above and so below represents the Law of Correspondence, so all bases are covered here.

WINTER MONEY SPELL

"To appreciate the beauty of a snowflake it is necessary to stand out in the cold." - Aristotle

Ingredients: Pine cones or pine needles, snow or an icicle, a clear glass jar, a silver coin

Moonphase: full

Step one: Place the pine cones or pine needles, the silver coin, and some snow or an icicle in the glass jar.

Step two: Place the jar outside where the moonlight can shine on the jar for 2 to 3 hours.

Step three: Bring the jar inside. It might be frozen. That's okay! Recite this spell as you focus on the jar:

"Winter moon and snowy pine

Bring the money that is mine

Melt my obstacles like the snow

As you let my income grow

By the power of three, so mote it be

For the good of all, it is done."

Step four: Place the jar on a windowsill overnight until everything is melted. Get excited about all the money and opportunities that are coming to you!

Step five: Empty the contents of the jar outside to return it to the earth. Keep the silver coin with you in a pocket or your purse at all times.

Why this works: This spell works in few ways. First, because you're harnessing natural materials and charging the snow or ice in the full moon, it has extra receptive power. Also, you're seeing the jar's contents melt, just like your obstacles to wealth. Pine trees are hearty and stay alive in even the coldest weather. Pine represents resilience, strength, rebirth and immortality.

One of my clients lives in Alaska where there's an abundance of snow. Claire shared her results with me after casting this spell: Her friend invited her on an outing and gave Claire the opportunity to try prospecting for gold. On her first time out, she found a nugget worth over $1300!

SPRING MONEY SPELL

"Spring is nature's way of saying, 'Let's Party!'" - Robin Williams

Ingredients: 3 Dandelions (the white fluffy kind), a yellow candle, a pinch of turmeric

Moonphase: waxing (getting bigger)

STEP ONE: RUB A BIT OF TURMERIC ON THE BASE OF YOUR YELLOW CANDLE AS YOU THINK OF

why you want to attract this money

For example: If I want to buy an RV, I'll think of driving the RV while I rub the turmeric on the base of the candle.

STEP TWO: LIGHT THE YELLOW CANDLE AND HOLD THE 3 DANDELIONS AS YOU SAY,

"Like the candle's flame of gold

With 3 blossoms I now hold

I draw to me the money I seek

With these words of power I speak

By the power of three, so mote it be."

STEP THREE: BLOW OUT THE CANDLE.

Step four: Go outside and blow the seeds off the dandelion heads one at a time, as you visualize spending the money on your desire you identified in step one. Thank the universe.

Why this works: Dandelion is associated with the planet Jupiter, which is also associated with good fortune and luck. As you blow the seeds off the flower, you are literally planting the seeds of your intentions! This is so potent. Yellow and turmeric are associated with the third (solar plexus) chakra, which is the chakra of personal power. This chakra will help you achieve your desires and goals.

One of my clients had a huge surge in confidence after casting this spell. She decided to finally launch a new book series she had been thinking about writing for while. Sarra sold thousands of copies the same day she released the first book.

SIMPLE AUTUMN MONEY SPELL

"Autumn is a second Spring when every leaf is a flower."- Albert Camus

Ingredients: A large bowl, 33 acorns, a silver coin, a clear glass jar, a green candle

Moonphase: Waxing or full

Step one: Go outside and gather 33 acorns. Acorns come from oak trees, so you will find an abundance of acorns near oaks.

Step two: Place the acorns and the silver coin in your jar. Place the jar outside to charge in the moonlight for up to 3 hours.

Step three: Bring your jar inside where you can look at it. Light your green candle

STEP FOUR: JOYFULLY SAY THE FOLLOWING SPELL:

"As above and so below

Money like these acorns grow

into large and healthy trees

Naturally and with ease

By the power of three, so mote it be"

Step five: Blow the candle out. Bury the acorns outside, knowing that as they grow, your wealth grows too. Keep your silver coin with you in a pocket or your purse.

My client Hannah closed on a real estate deal after casting this spell. She earned over $200,000.

Why this works: You're combining the power of nature with the power of your intentions. Acorns come from oak trees. Oak represents good luck, success, money, strength and protection.

SUMMER MONEY SPELL JAR

"And so with the sunshine and the great bursts of leaves growing on the trees, just as things grow in fast movies, I had that familiar conviction that life was beginning over again with the summer."- F. Scott Fitzgerald, The Great Gatsby

Ingredients: 3 seashells from your favorite beach, a sheet of paper, a green pen or marker, 33 pennies

Optional ingredients: 3 pieces of citrine

Step one: Using your green pen, write your intention on the piece of paper. For example: "I intend to visit Europe in the year 2020. Thank you for bringing me all the resources for the trip."

Step two: Fold the slip of paper and put it in the jar. Put the pennies and shells on top of the paper as you imagine yourself reaching your goal. In my case, I'd imagine myself going on the trip. I'd believe it and start planning for it.

STEP THREE: HOLD THE JAR IN YOUR HANDS AS YOU SAY:

"Toward my wish this money flows

Everyday it grows and grows

Thank you for the coins I see

And for all the money that comes to me

By the power of three, so mote it be."

Step four: Keep the jar on a sunny windowsill. This jar is your new piggy bank. Whenever you get spare change, throw it in the jar and thank the universe. If you throw change in it everyday, the more powerful this spell becomes.

My client Daniella said she loves this spell because she's a visual person. Seeing the money grow and increase daily really helped anchor in the good feelings. She had tremendous results with this spell...She sold 5 large paintings to an art collector within 3 weeks.

Why this works: You're literally seeing your money grow every day in the jar. The coins and shells are literally on top of your wish (goal paper). The sun is charging them with fresh energy each day. Copper (pennies) relates to the solar plexus Chakra for will power and confidence.

After you reach the goal you wrote down, thank the universe and spend, donate or deposit the coins in the jar. You can do this spell again with a new goal or intention (and new coins) after you reach the first goal you've written.

EASY MONEY SPELL

"Why Worry? What is meant for you is always meant to find you. —Indian poet-saint Lalleshwari"

Ingredients: A green candle, a sheet of paper and a pen, a silver coin

Moon Phase: any

STEP ONE: THINK OF THE AMOUNT OF MONEY YOU ARE REQUESTING AND WHY YOU NEED IT

Example: "$850 for Mortgage Payment"

STEP TWO: WRITE THAT AMOUNT ON THE SHEET OF PAPER

STEP THREE: CARVE THE CURRENCY SYMBOL ($ FOR USA) INTO THE CANDLE WITH THE COIN

STEP FOUR: LIGHT THE CANDLE AND FOCUS ON YOUR INTENTION FOR THE SPELL FOR 10 MINUTES. IMAGINE RECEIVING THE MONEY AND USING IT FOR THE PURPOSE YOUR REQUESTED IT FOR.

STEP FIVE: SAY THESE WORDS:

"Easy money come to me

With harm to none

So mote it be."

Step Six: Pour some of the wax from the candle on the the sheet of paper. Fold the paper up and keep it with the coin in your pocket or wallet until you receive the money. Blow the candle out.

Optional: You can relight the candle every day for up to 7 days (repeating steps 4 through 6).

My friend is a freelancer and swears by this spell to keep the clients (and money) flowing.

Why this works: Writing your goal activates your RSA (Reticular Activating System) and impresses your goal onto your subconscious mind. Using the coin to carve the currency symbol does this too and charges the candle with your intentions.

MIRROR WALLET MONEY SPELL

"There are two ways of spreading light: to be the candle or the mirror that reflects it." Edith Wharton

Ingredients: a pocket mirror, dollar bills, your wallet

Moon phase: Any

DAY OF THE WEEK TO START: START THIS SPELL ON A THURSDAY (FOR JUPITER'S LUCKY INFLUENCE)

Step one: Place the dollar bills in your wallet. Place the pocket mirror next to them. Always keep dollars in your wallet with the mirror.

STEP TWO: SAY THIS:

"As I sleep, Ideas come

To multiply my income

With harm to none

And wealth to all

By the power of three

So mote it be."

Step three: Keep the mirror and the dollars in your wallet.

Why this works: A mirror appears to multiply whatever you put in front of it, so you get to actually SEE your money doubled. Seeing is believing.

GROWING MONEY SPELL

Quote: "If you have a garden and a library, you have everything you need."- Marcus Tullius Cicero

Ingredients: a quarter, a fancy wine glass, a cup of water

Moonphase: Full

Step one: Fill your wine glass with water and place your silver coin in it. Position your glass so that light of the full moon can shine through it for 30 minutes. You may have to put the glass outside.

STEP TWO: SAY THIS AS YOU LOOK AT YOUR GLASS AND FOCUS ON YOUR INTENTION:

"Gorgeous moon, hear my spell

Fill this cup up like a well

As above, so below

Make my income grow and grow."

Step three: Go outside and bury the coin directly across from the front door of your house. Water the coin with the water from your wine glass.

Optional: Plant flower seeds with your coin to really see your income blossom.

Why this works: We know we must plant trees, vegetables and such in order for them to grow. We send a powerful message to our subconscious mind about our incoming growing when we cast this spell. The full moon helps charge the ingredients and your intentions.

REFUND FROM THE UNIVERSE SPELL

"Each moment of our life, we either invoke or destroy our dreams. We call upon it to become a fact, or we cancel our previous instructions." Stuart Wilde

This spell is from Stuart Wilde's fantastic "Little Money Bible" book.

Ingredients: a white candle, a sheet of paper and a writing utensil

Moonphase: any

Step one: Think about all the kind things you've done over the last year. Perhaps you've donated your time to a charity or cause. Perhaps you've donated trash bags full of stuff to Goodwill or another thrift shop. Maybe you've smiled at a stranger or bought someone coffee. Maybe you helped someone move or gave a sincere compliment to someone in need. Maybe you helped a neighbor out with something.

Step two: You did all these kindnesses without asking to be compensated. And since you've put in a lot of time and energy, the universe will give you an energetic REFUND. But only if you ask for it.

Step three: Light the candle and write a letter to the universe asking to be paid back for all the energy you've put out into the world. Expect a pay off.

Side note: Stuart suggests you keep this candle burning constantly for 7 days, but since I don't want you to start a fire, I suggest you follow basic safety precautions and simply light the candle once a day for 7 days like I did. The spell will still work. My friend who volunteers at a school out of the kindness of her heart did this spell and won $350 the same night.

Within 3 weeks of casting this spell, I received a check in the mail, a few new clients and a vacation...all worth over $5000.

PART 2: RICH WITCH HABITS

RICH WITCH HABITS

What are Habits?

Before we dive into the rich witch habits, let's first define what a habit is.

A habit is something you do automatically without even thinking. For example, you might automatically lock the door when you get home. Maybe you've accidentally locked your partner out when they stepped outside to walk the dog because you don't even think about locking the door anymore. Your brain just locks the door on autopilot.

Another habit might be brushing your teeth when you wake up. This was a habit you learned. At first, maybe your parents had to remind you to brush your teeth every day when you were a kid. But eventually, brushing your teeth became a habit. Similarly, the habits in this section are all learnable. Practice the following habits enough and they will feel as natural to you as brushing your teeth in the morning.

Here's a little warning, when you get really busy or stressed out, your new wealth habits will be the first thing you forget. It happens to all of us. Don't freak out. Just be aware of it so you can get back on track as soon as possible.

GRATITUDE

"Fulfillment isn't found over the rainbow—it's found in the here and now. Today I define success by the fluidity with which I transcend emotional landmines and choose joy and gratitude instead." RuPaul

Rich Witches know that in order to have more money, they must APPRECIATE the money, stuff, friends (and everything!) that's already in their lives. The energy of appreciation is magnetic. Find the feeling of being rich and grateful NOW. If you tell the universe you don't have enough, it will mirror that back to you.

When you train an animal, you train him or her by giving them positive reinforcement in the form of a treat. You praise the animal. You say 'thank you' to him or her. You pet them and tell them they did a good job. This motivates them to please you and do as you ask.

Imagine money was the animal and you said to him or her, "you're nothing to me" or "I hate you" or "you don't matter" or "you're the root of all evil…."

Would you expect the animal (or money) to listen to you or stick around?!

No way! Similarly, You have to show MONEY that you are grateful by appreciating it, taking care of it, and giving it space when needed. It's all about balance. That means you aren't afraid to spend some money when you need to, and that you don't go blowing ALL of your money at once either.

How to practice gratitude other than saying thank you?

You can start and keep a gratitude journal and write 3 things you appreciate every day. This habit will literally train your brain to look for things to be grateful for, which will help you create and align with even more things to be grateful for.

You can create a gratitude jar. Take a clear glass jar and a stack of post-its. Each day, write something you're grateful for and put it in the jar. When you need a boost of positive energy, read the notes in the jar or flip through your gratitude journal. I love reading all the great things that happened in my gratitude jar. I make it an annual New Year's day practice.

My client Sylvia did this and she said it helped her grow her jewelry business better than any marketing plan she ever tried. Try it for yourself and see.

RICH WITCH MORNING

"This is a wonderful day. I've never seen this one before." Maya Angelou

Rich Witches (and most successful people) have a morning routine. No, this doesn't mean you have to get up earlier than everyone else on the planet. I love to sleep late when I can! However, it is important that you are intentional about what you do first thing in the morning. Why? Because it sets the tone for the rest of the day.

In the past, I used to spend far too much time on morning chores. Starting my day off with washing dirty dishes and doing laundry took up my valuable time and energy that I could've spent on yoga or writing and other enjoyable things. I was exhausted by the time I needed to write! Putting chores first also lowered my mood and made me feel like chores were neverending. It was not a great way to start the day!

And so I made a change. Saving chores for last ensured that I had the energy to do what is most important first.

What do you do first thing in the morning?

If you grab your phone first thing in the morning and start scrolling through Social Media, you train your brain to zone out and be distracted. You also send a message to your subconscious mind that says, "everything else is more important than me."

How on earth can you expect your spells to be powerful if you are zoned out, distracted and feel like you don't matter?

Perhaps you have to put your babies or kids (or pets) first. But please don't put your phone first.

Your subconscious mind is extra active in the morning, so feed it some affirmations or show yourself that you matter by practicing self-care first thing in the morning. More on Self-Care in the next section.

Maybe you have to get up super early for work and you feel like a zombie. I get it. That used to be me. But what one small tweak can you make to your morning to show yourself that you are *worth being treated well?*

If you are neglecting yourself, you cannot expect anyone else to give you attention. And you can't expect money to pay attention to you either.

MANAGE YOUR TIME

"Either run the day or the day runs you." - Jim Rohn

If you have an important goal, project or priority, schedule it on your calendar everyday. Make the time for it. If you don't put it on your schedule or planner, you will forget to do it.

If you really want to do something, you'll find a way. For example, I'm writing this book while I'm on vacation. This is what's fun for me. If I was at home, I know chores and other obligations would get in the way.

Don't lie to yourself by saying you don't have time. This only holds you back. How can you make the time? Rich witches and other successful people make the time by cutting out distractions.

My husband works 40 hours every week. He still works out for an hour every single day. He doesn't make the excuse that he's too busy or too tired. It's really inspiring to me.

Here are some ideas for you to create more time in your schedule:
- Quit social media temporarily (or forever)
- Stop watching TV until you finish your project
- Work on your priority in the morning

- Work on your priority in the evening
- Work on your priority on your lunch break
- Delegate a chore to someone else so you can work on your priority

SELF-CARE

"If you can't love yourself, how the hell are you gonna love somebody else?"- RuPaul

The phrase "self care" is pretty triggering for many women. Especially since most of us were taught to care about everyone else first. Pro-tip, people who call you "selfish" for taking care of yourself usually want to manipulate you into doing something *for them*.

But a rich witch knows that she can't help anyone if she is overworked, running around ragged, and putting herself dead last. Like the phrase goes, "you can't pour from an empty cup."

Unfortunately, prioritizing myself was a lesson I had to learn the hard way. And it's a lesson that I sometimes forget when my schedule fills up. Can you relate?

Recently I had to go to urgent care for stomach pains that were so intense I nearly passed out in the exam room. But before I even mentioned the pain to my husband, I did the dishes and mopped the floor and took care of two dogs. I was silently screaming at myself in my head the whole time, "Zelda, what the heck are you doing? Ask for help!"

I don't know why I didn't ask for help. It was an old habit for me to push through and deal with the pain rather than sit down and relax. Of course this experience was a powerful lesson. My intuition was screaming at me via my body and I just wasn't listening.

I'm sure you've probably heard the airplane oxygen mask warning before. Just in case you haven't, I'll share it with you. When you fly in an airplane, you get a warning that if there's an emergency, **you have to put on your own oxygen mask FIRST**...because you can't help your kids or loved ones if you are passed out or dead.

Self-care goes beyond just taking a bubble bath (although I LOVE baths, especially magical baths). Sometimes self-care means saying NO and being honest even if it's uncomfortable.

How to practice self care?

From now on, treat yourself like you would treat your pet, a beloved child or best friend. This is easier said than done if you've been beating yourself up for years. But it's possible. Start small.

Step one: Make a list of things you wish you had time for. Maybe you want to work out a few times a week, get a monthly massage, go on a trip, or just have a nice cup of tea every day for 10 minutes. Write it all down, even if it seems unrealistic.

Step two: Say "no" to things that aren't on your list. That's it.

PLAY

"Play isn't something separate from the daily grind of life. It is not something to finally get to when work ends. Rather, play, like music, is a force that we feel in our bones and that whispers in our heart. As kids demonstrate, play is not over there, but forever here and now." ~ Vince Gowmon

Have you ever noticed that the word FUND contains FUN? Thanks to Star Khechara for showing me that :) It's not a coincidence. When you are having fun, you are raising your energy. That is the key to powerful spells and abundance. Lots of energy = lots of money, opportunities, and ideas. On the other hand, if you have the energy of a garden slug, you will receive way less ideas, far less opportunities, and you probably need a nap instead of cash.

Don't skip this! I know some of you die-hard workaholics are probably rolling your eyes. I promise the results of allowing yourself to play are worth it. Try it out for yourself.

Some of you are probably chucking because you feel you don't have enough time to play. Can you see the irony in that? If you don't feel you have ENOUGH time, does that sound like a mindset of abundance to you? I rest my case.

Rich Witches know that play and fun are not just for children. In fact, our inner children are alive and well. They are inside of us right now. This is not woo-woo nonsense, but a powerful Psychological reality.

A friend of mine who owns a successful business was panicking because she was about to go on vacation. "I don't have paid days off like regular full-timers," she said. Sabrina was afraid that while she was gone, she wouldn't make any money because she'd having fun instead of grinding away at the computer. I finally convinced Sabrina that her business would be okay for a week….and that seven days off was not going to make business dry up or all of her clients run away. On the flip side, all that the fun she'd have on her trip might actually help her business, not hurt it.

When Sabrina returned the following week, she called to tell me she actually booked several new clients while she was out hiking the gorgeous Mountains of Iceland.

In her book the Artist's Way, Julia Cameron encourages the reader to go out on an "Artist's Date" once a week. On an Artist's date, you go out alone without a plan or an agenda. On an artist's date, you also allow your inner child to pick out a souvenir to bring home with you. I bought my inner child bubbles and a piggy bank recently. You may end up at the park. You might end up taking a train to new city. The point of the artist date is to give yourself the freedom the to play so that you can be more creative.

Anyone and everyone can benefit from the Artist's date, not just artists. Why? Because taking yourself out on a date with no plans *is fun*! I always come up with lucrative ideas when I'm on my artist's dates. You're reading one of them right now.

Do something fun today! Zelda's orders.

Need some ideas? Blow bubbles. Play with playdough or silly puddy. Make a sand castle. Finger paint. Hula hoop. Jump rope. Play hopscotch. Visit a playground and swing on the swings. Play a board game or video game you enjoyed as a kid. Hug a stuffed animal. Play with your pet. Doodle. Draw. Play!

SAY NO TO GRUDGES

"Holding onto anger is like drinking poison and expecting the other person to die."- Source Unknown

Rich witches don't hold grudges because they know grudges are a waste of energy. I grew up in a home where certain people around me held grudges. As a result, I had to teach myself how to handle conflict when I became an adult. If I can do it, so can you.

"Would you rather be right or rich?" Denise Duffield Thomas

When you have anger or resentment, you're putting a TON of energy and focus toward negativity instead of being happy or building your empire. But resentment doesn't really punish the other person. Instead it drags YOU down.

"If you want to be successful, you need to study success, not hate it or be envious of it. If you are envious, you will distance yourself from success and make it that much harder to get there. Never be jealous or think someone is lucky. Luck is created by the prepared."- James Altucher

What if you have resentment? Brad Yates has an amazing (and so effective) EFT video for free on his Youtube Channel. Give it a search.

I received an unexpected check in the mail after following along with the video I mentioned above. You might say that's a coincidence, but it can't hurt to try. What have you got to lose?

"You can't create what you hate." -Hawaiian Huna Philosophy

Do you find yourself envying people who have what you want? If so, you are pushing that very thing you desire AWAY from you! So what do you do when the green-eyed monster (AKA Jealousy) rears its head? You can find a Brad Yates EFT video about jealousy, or you can break out the big guns...

Ho'oponopono is a forgiveness technique made popular by Joe Vitale, but it comes from ancient Hawaiian history. More on the technique in a moment.

Dr. Hew Len was summoned by a mental institution for extremely dangerous criminals. He rarely had direct contact with them. Instead, he would do the Ho'oponopono mantra on their files. Within 4 years of Len working there, the hospital had to close because most of the criminals were no longer dangerous or mentally ill. They had to be released. But how?

Dr. Len explained that he was healing the part of him that created the criminals. By working on himself, he changed the people around him. Remember, the universe is like a mirror.

It might sound off the wall or outrageous to you, but the world around you is a reflection of you. Trying to change the world is like trying to change the mirror and expecting yourself to change. You have to change yourself, then the reflection changes.

The forgiveness mantra used my Dr. Len and millions of others is: "I love You, I'm sorry, Please forgive me, Thank You."

When I say this mantra, I imagine I am saying all these words (especially "I'm sorry") to myself for getting myself into this mess to begin with. I recently did this mantra on someone I was mad at. I received an out of the blue check in the mail from that person the next day!

SAY NO TO TOXIC PEOPLE

"You're the average of the five people spend the most time with."- Jim Rohn

Avoiding grudges is so much easier if you aren't hanging around with toxic people. I know that term is harsh. Your intuition will tell you who is good for you and who isn't, so make sure you listen.

How can you tell someone is not good for you to be around? Usually you will know AFTER you spent time with them.

You might feel:
- Drained
- Exhausted
- Angry, Annoyed
- In a bad mood for no reason

Even if the person seems "nice", if you feel awful after spending time with them, you need to decrease the amount of time you spend with them for your own good. It's tough, but you have to protect yourself and your energy or your spells will be useless. Your energy is precious, so spend it wisely.

Suppose that not-good-for-you-person is a family member or in-law and you have to see them sometimes.

Prepare for it by setting boundaries (more on that in the next section) and sticking those boundaries. Remember, "no" is a complete sentence.

Take an epsom salt bath (or salt scrub in the shower if you don't have a tub) and sage yourself after you are around that person. The salt will draw out any energy that doesn't belong to you. The sage will cleanse your energy field.

Many techniques for empaths will advise you to try to block out the other person's energy. Unfortunately, what you resist persists, so this does not work. What to do instead?

The Keyhole Technique

I learned this from a healer whose name I can't recall at the moment. You need to imagine your heart has a keyhole in it when you are with that certain person or group of people. Then you say in your mind, "I am me and you are you, all of your energy goes right through."

I use this with the people I'd rather not interact with and it works like a charm.

My client Joanna was ready to stop hanging out with a certain person who drained her. I gave her the tips you just read. She texted me a month later to tell me how much happier and freer she felt. Not only that, but she even got a raise at work because her manager noticed the positive changes she was making.

MAKE IT NORMAL FOR YOU

Surrounding yourself with people who inspire you will *normalize success and wealth for you.*

Have you ever felt yourself doing something you wouldn't ordinarily do when you're around certain people?

For example, eating healthy is very important to me. However, when I visit certain people and see wall-to-wall Oreos, candy and cheese in their house, I get tempted. It becomes harder to stick to my way of eating. So I have to either invite them to my house or limit the time I spend in their home.

People are social creatures. This is why it's important to be intentional about who you spend your time with. If you spend time with people who are improving their lives, you will most likely start to improve your life as well.

On the flip side, if all of your friends are constantly complaining about everything and gossiping on a regular basis, what do you think you're going to be tempted to do when you hang out with them? Even if you don't do what they do, their energy will drag you down.

I'm not suggesting you dump all of your friends, but to be aware of how they are impacting you. Seek out friends who have similar values. Decrease the amount of time you spend with people you wouldn't want to trade places with.

My client Tina was ready to make success normal for her. She was sick of hearing her friends complain about money all the time and tired of seeing them stagnate. Tina made a change. She took a painting class, joined a new meetup group, and started to make new friends. She texted me 3 weeks later to tell me that she was offered a job as an art assistant, got to go sailing on her new friend's boat, and is feeling better than she has in years. She's feeling wealthier and attracting new opportunities as a result.

A big reason why you aren't already rich is because it would be too different and too abnormal for you. Think about it. Are you afraid of earning more than a certain someone? Of leaving someone "behind?" Women often keep themselves small because they don't want to outshine anyone. But a rich witch doesn't make herself smaller, instead she EXPANDS and seeks friends who are improving their lives.

How to make success and wealth feel NORMAL for you:

- Go where wealthy people go: spend time in a fancy tea or coffee shop. Or visit the lobby of a fancy hotel. Normalize it.
- Read a biography of a rich person you admire
- Expand your social circle

- Take a class or read a book by someone who inspires you

BOUNDARIES

**"Givers need to set limits because takers rarely do."-
Rachel Wolchin**

Most people think boundaries are for other people.
Actually, boundaries are set by you and enforced by you.
Nobody can stomp all over your boundaries without your
permission. Rich witches know what their boundaries are
and enforce them.

My Dad recently warned me to never accept a breath
mint from a stranger because the latest "thing" is
poisoned or roofied mints. My response? "I'd never allow
a stranger to get close enough to smell my breath
anyway. Plus, if a stranger stands too close to me or tries
to enter my bubble, I'd move back or leave." Boundaries
for the win.

You will know if someone violates your boundaries
because you will feel just plain bad as a result.

Most people don't enforce their boundaries because they
are afraid of rejection or hurting others' feelings. People
who lack boundaries feel responsible for how other
people feel. But a rich witch knows that her own opinion
of herself is far more important than what other people
(especially takers and boundary stompers) think of her.

There are a few different types of boundaries, including physical, personal and emotional. The Dad mint story above was an example of a physical boundary.

Only you can define your boundaries and follow them. If you have weak boundaries (as in "people pleasing"), people will sense this and take advantage of you. I swear, people have some kind of radar and can always tell. They try to tell my husband all of their sob stories.

If you want to watch an awful movie about what happens when you don't have boundaries, watch "Mother," starring Jennifer Lawrence. Don't say I didn't warn you. This movie is not a feel-good movie.

How to Create Boundaries

Don't say "yes" when you want to say "no". Don't say "no" when you want to say "yes".

Here's another idea: Write a list of things you will no longer tolerate anymore. Stick to it!
For example, my physical boundary is that if someone in a public place starts smoking a cigarette, I leave.

Setting boundaries in your relationships is up to you.

Here's another example. Up until recently, my mom constantly posted terrible news stories about animal attacks on my Facebook wall until I asked her to stop. She listened to me for a few weeks. When she had a momentary slip up and texted me a terrible news story, I didn't get mad. Instead I told her what would happen if she did it again. And because she didn't want me to block her, she followed my boundary. But first I followed it myself by speaking up about it.

What do boundaries have to do with money?

Everything! Want to know why? Because most of the time, the money you get will come from other people in some form.

If you're the type of person who has trouble saying "no" to other people, you will be tempted to work for free or run yourself into the ground. You'll be tempted to discount your services to death or say yes to the wrong clients, or put everyone else's needs ahead of your own until you have no energy left. And money is a form of energy. It's all connected.

"Every time you say yes to something you don't want to do, this will happen: you will resent people, you will do a bad job, you will have less energy for the things you were doing a good job on, you will make less money, and yet another small percentage of your life will be used up, burned up, a smoke signal to the future saying, "I did it again."
— **James Altucher, Choose Yourself**

FOLLOW YOUR INTUITION

"Intuition is a gut feeling—or a hunch— a sensation that appears quickly in consciousness (noticeable enough to be acted on if one chooses to) without us being fully aware of the underlying reasons for its occurrence."- Francis Cholle

Rich witches follow their intuition. Following your intuition can help you make money or find hidden treasures.

One day I decided to visit an out-of-the-way coffee shop in a different side of town. I'd normally go to a closer coffee shop, but my intuition was telling me to shake up my routine. After I got my tea, I was so content and just enjoying my delicious chai, walking around the parking lot and taking my time. My intuition steered me next to the parking lot off the sidewalk. That's when I looked down and saw a gorgeous opal ring glittering in the sunlight.

Your intuition can help you find lost objects and money, but more importantly, it can also help you avoid bad decisions. Your intuition might help save your life!

I was driving on a busy highway during a road trip a few years ago. The sun was shining and the music was playing. Out of nowhere, I had the sudden urge to immediately switch lanes and pass a giant semi truck that was to my left. I didn't see any logical reason to change lanes, but I followed my intuition anyway. As soon as I moved my car into the left lane, the giant semi-truck that was next to my car a second before sped into the right lane without warning. If I didn't change lanes, they would have crashed into my car or ran me off the road.

How many times have you ignored your intuition screaming at you, only to end up wishing you had listened to yourself? Up until recently, I have done that too many times to count.

"Intuition is always right in at least two important ways; It is always a response to something. And it always has your best interest at heart." -Gavin De Becker, The Gift of Fear

How to listen to your intuition?

If you aren't used to listening to your intuition, here are a few pointers to help you learn how to listen.

- Spend quiet time alone daily. Your intuition is much harder to hear if you are always surrounded by noise. Distraction also makes it harder to hear, so ease up on multitasking.
- Go out in nature. You don't have to become a farmer, but just being outside will help you connect to yourself. We ARE nature.
- Practice Meditation. Start by doing a guided meditation on Youtube to quiet your mind. Or do a

walking meditation and simply focus on the sounds you hear, the things you see, and all the smells you smell at your local park.

● Clear your thoughts by journaling. A quiet mind is a receptive mind.

● Notice synchronicities and "coincidences" when they occur to increase them.

LEAVE YOUR COMFORT ZONE

"Insanity is doing the same thing and expecting different results" - Albert Einstein

Routines feel familiar and "safe." I get it. But If you want your life or your income to change, you have to take the first step and actually do something different. Most people drive the same way to work all the time, eat the same meals week after week, and hang out with the same people over and over again. As a result, their lives don't really change much, even when they want to change. It's like living on autopilot.

I have a client who forces herself to skydive, bungee jumping and do all kinds of scary thrill-seeking stuff, but she is still stuck in the same old mindset and daily routine. Amy (not her real name) eats the same foods everyday. She goes to the same places on the weekends. She talks about the same stuff all the time. Amy won't try a new meal or place to eat. And she is deathly afraid of any type of criticism. But it's not Amy's fault...

It's not Amy's fault because her brain is just trying to keep her safe. You see, your brain wasn't meant to make you happy or rich. Your brain's only job is to keep you alive. So anything that threatens your cozy little "safe" comfort zone is seen as dangerous and even deadly.

Because in the recent past, being a powerful woman was deadly! Afterall, not too long ago, women were burned at the stake for being powerful.

When a woman steps into her power and feels that deathly fear of being seen or criticized, she is also dealing with fears and traumas passed down through generations. This is the entire reason I wrote my book series under a pen name…my real name is Sarah.

Kimberly Jones refers to this fear as **the "witch wound."** She eloquently states:

"The Witch Wound is what pits women against each other, competing and comparing one another, stealing each other's ideas and dishonouring each other. It is the fear that arises when one of our friends, relatives or colleagues opens up about their psychic gifts or interests and we freak out and start judging and shaming them (not wishing to be tarred with the witchy brush and sent to the gallows alongside them). The Patriarchy perpetuates the wider Witch Wound, it controls through fear."

Another client, Betty, decided to shake up her routine in a big way. She worked close enough to home that she could ride a bike to the salon, but she didn't have a bike yet. So Betty's sister loaned her a bike until she could buy the electric bike she wanted. Betty decided to imagine she was on her new electric bike every time she pedaled her sister's old bike. Within a week, she got the urge to take a different route to work. Betty listened to her intuition and found a lost dog wearing a collar on the way. She stopped and the dog walked right up to her.

Betty called the phone number on the tag. The dog's owner was so thrilled that she gave Betty a reward for reuniting Rosie with her owner. It was enough to buy her own electric bike.

Rich witches know that comfort zones only produce *comfort*, not mindblowing results. If you want to have more abundance, you need to switch up your *routine* once in a while and swim outside of your comfort zone. For best results, you have to change something that you normally do everyday.

"I've been absolutely terrified every moment of my life - and I've never let it keep me from doing a single thing I wanted to do." -Georgia O'Keeffe

Here's why: When you allow yourself to venture outside of the familiar, the universe will reward you with fresh ideas, new results, and new experiences. Even your brain responds by producing new neural pathways, which makes you smarter, fends off Alzheimer's disease, and allows you to see your life in a new way. New perspective = new money-making ideas!

Try something new today! Try something new every day of this week.

Here's a few ideas to get you started: Try a new restaurant. Order something you've never tasted before. Wear a style of clothing or color you've never dared to wear before. Go to a new meetup group. Go somewhere in your town you've never been before. Try a new hobby that you've never thought to try before. Experiment, experiment, experiment.

ASK FOR HELP

"The strong individual is one who asks for help when she needs it." - Rona Barrett

Up until recently, I would rarely ask for help. In fact, I had a block about receiving help because I saw a lot of people who took advantage of others and acted like total needy babies who couldn't do anything for themselves. It was really unattractive in my opinion. So I swung in the opposite direction at the other end of the spectrum. Until I realized that the *opposite* of asking for others to do everything (doing it all myself) wasn't healthy either. Now I've settled into a more balanced happy midpoint where I sometimes ask for help if I need it.

Rich witches know that asking for help isn't a weakness. If you try to do everything yourself, you miss out on opportunities for the universe to help you. You will also end up feeling depleted and resentful...not abundant!

You may feel like nobody else can do it all as well as you. If this is the case, you may need to loosen the reins. Trying to control everything is a sign that you need to exercise your trust muscle.

On the other hand, you may try to do it all yourself because you're afraid people will say "no" if you ask. Ask anyway. The rich witch doesn't let a fear of rejection force her into doing it all alone.

Another reason to ask for help is to show yourself how we are all connected and how we all benefit from cooperation. Cooperation is the antidote to scarcity.

"Alone we can do so little. Together we can do so much." - Helen Keller

The next time you eat an apple, think of all the people it took to produce it. Someone had to plant the seed. Someone had to take care of the apple tree and make sure it had enough sun and water. Someone had to pick the apple. Someone else drove it to the Farmer's Market or Grocery Store.

In fact, most products, buildings, books, etc. are the result of a collaboration of some sort.

So what can you delegate or ask for help with today?

Is there something you've been wanting to create but don't know how? I bet you might know someone who does. Accepting help tells the universe you are ready to receive more.

WORTHINESS

"Give it to me, I'm worth it."- Fifth Harmony

Many women believe their worth or value stems from what they can give or do for someone else. They believe that in order to receive money or love, they have to first do something. It's transactional. So they work themselves into exhaustion or give far too much in order to deserve. These women (and men) are prone to becoming workaholics. In a love relationship, these women give far too much and end up feeling resentful because their partner doesn't give as much as she does.

One of my clients, Patricia, had the belief that she wasn't worth anything unless she was busy all the time. You can probably already guess that Patricia was chronically exhausted, and as a result, she was repelling opportunities and money. Eventually Patricia got fed up and decided to make a change. Patricia started treating herself better. She eventually asked for a raise at work, believing she was truly worth it. When her boss said "no," she found another job with a pay rate that matched her new worthiness.

Rich witches know they are worthy, period. If you're reading this, you're worthy too. You don't have to work hard for it. You are worthy just because you exist. You already deserve to receive what you desire. You don't have to work yourself into exhaustion or beg or overdeliver. The only thing you have to do is *take action*.

And taking action is what separates those who know they are worthy and those who feel entitled (on the other end of the spectrum). People who feel entitled have an exaggerated sense of deserving that stems from low self-esteem or a belief that they are incapable. This is not what we're going for at all. These people expect the universe and other people to do everything and provide everything for them. These people always aim to seek out people with poor boundaries so they can mooch off of them like a blood sucking leach. This is not rich witch behavior.

Do you need to work on feeling worthy? Feeling like you don't deserve to get what you want is a way to block it from showing up in your life.

Treat yourself like the Goddess you are. Raise your standards and don't settle. Don't allow people to mistreat you or underpay you.

LET YOURSELF RECEIVE

"You only get what you have the capacity to receive."-Maru Iabichela

Rich witches allow other people the joy of giving to them. They don't feel guilty accepting gifts or compliments. And they don't feel like they immediately owe the giver something in return.

The good news is that if you have a tough time accepting gifts and compliments, it's a skill you can learn. I was raised to feel guilty if somebody did something nice for me. But I changed that belief because I realized I deserve kindness.

Have you ever complimented someone's outfit and they responded, "oh, this shirt is so old" instead of saying thank you? It makes you feel like you don't want to compliment them anymore.

Maru Iabichela, the creator of Infinite Receiving, taught me that when you graciously accept gifts and compliments from people, the universe will be generous to you as well. But if you constantly say, "not thanks," or you explain away compliments, the universe will assume you don't want to receive and will give the money, raises, opportunities (and more) to someone else.

Start activating your receiving power right now: Sign up to receive a free digital copy when I release my next book: http://tinyurl.com/zeldabarrons

TAKE RESPONSIBILITY

"Excuses are leaks in a boat. When you cover one, another pops up, and it's even bigger. It's hard to keep the boat repaired and get safely to shore if you have an excuse mindset." — James Altucher, The Power of No: Because One Little Word Can Bring Health, Abundance, and Happiness

Do you know someone who blames everyone else for the circumstances in their lives? With this person, it's always someone else's fault. They blame the economy or their parents or the president and the list goes on and on. Blaming is draining and lowers your vibration. It's also draining for the people around you. Blaming takes your power away. Excuses only hold you back.

Rich witches take responsibility for their actions and for their lives. Taking responsibility gives you tremendous power...the power to change you or your circumstances if you desire! Never make yourself the victim of circumstances.

Common excuses to remove from your vocabulary:
- I'm too old to…
- I'm not old enough to…
- I'm not qualified for….
- I'm too tired to…

- Nobody will buy this…
- I don't have time to...
- People won't like it if I...

When the economy crashed in 2008, one of my clients was worried sick. So I reminded Samanta that there are still people doing quite well financially no matter what the economy is doing. If one source of money goes away, you can always find another one. And I asked Samantha to start looking for evidence of people who were still doing well financially.

The next time we talked, Samantha informed me she had started a new business online...and she gleefully admitted she was making more money than she ever made at her old office job. If Samantha had sat around blaming and worrying, she never would have gotten started. Instead, she took matters into her own hands. She took responsibility and power over the situation.

ALWAYS BE LEARNING

"The day we stop learning is the day we die." - Michael Scott, *The Office*

Rich witches are humble enough to admit when they don't know something. They are open to learning new things and new ways of doing things. There's no harm in trying. If you treat every interaction with someone as an opportunity to learn something, you will add so much value to your life.

There's no excuse not to learn. Libraries are free. If you're reading this, Google and YouTube are at your fingertips. After all, learning from someone else who has already achieved what you want to accomplish is the fastest shortcut there is.

When we learn, our brains actually change. This is called plasticity of the brain. The brain that changes is more open to seeing all the opportunities out there. And opportunities lead to money in the bank.

"I have never met a mentally strong person who wasn't a voracious reader." **— James Altucher, The Rich Employee**

Learn something new today.

TREAT YOUR MONEY WELL

"Take care of the little things and the big things will take care of themselves. You gain control over your life by paying closer attention to the small things." - Emily Dickinson

Clean out your wallet and purse. Throw away old receipts from 10 years ago. When you throw away what is no longer needed, you create space for more. You create room for ease and flow. Your wallet and purse are where money lives...give it a nice home to live in!

How you treat money plays a factor in how much you have. Imagine if money was a person who saw you crumbling up dollar bills in a wadded mess in your pocket. If money saw you treating money that way, do you think it would want to be treated like that? Make sure your dollar bills are neat and all facing the same way in your wallet.

One of my clients admitted she was messy and had trouble keeping track of her money. Janel wasn't kidding. Not only did she have a lot of clutter, receipts and trash in her apartment, but there were coins all over the place! There were dozens of pennies on the floor in random piles, piles of quarters in the bathroom and on the kitchen counters. I couldn't imagine why anyone would just let money lay around on the floor like that. We collected it all in a glass jar and cashed it in at a Coinstar machine. Janel had over $100 in change laying around her apartment!

I informed Janel that if she treated money better, money would be more willing to hang around. She was skeptical but willing to make a change. She bought a giant piggy bank in the kid's department of Target. This piggy bank now lives on Janel's coffee table. Not only does Janel "feed her piggy" daily, but whenever friends visit her apartment, they love dumping their change into the piggy bank too.

SAVE A PERCENTAGE OF EVERYTHING YOU EARN

"People have got to learn: if they don't have cookies in the cookie jar, they can't eat cookies."- Suze Orman

So far we've talked mostly about metaphysical ways to align with more wealth. But Madonna was right...this is also a material world we are living in. So this practical tip has you covered.

I learned this lesson the hard way. I used to earn over $100 per hour...but I never kept any of it. The truth is, deep down I felt like I wasn't worthy of the money. So no matter how much I made, I always found a way to get rid of it. I'd overspend on courses I didn't need or didn't even use. Luckily I realized my blunder. Although I earned less per hour last year, I kept way more of the money.

No matter how much money you earn, if you *always keep some of it*, you will ALWAYS have money. It's a simple concept that even some of the smartest people fail to realize.

One of my clients |(name withheld) used to chase after "get rich quick schemes" and throw away a ton of money that way. If she'd get a stable job making even modest pay and save some of her income each month, she'd be much further along than she is now.

On the other hand, I have a client who is pretty balanced with her spending and saving. She doesn't make that much money compared to some people, but she saves a big portion of her pay. And so she always has money.

DON'T COMPARE YOURSELF TO OTHERS

"Only compare yourself to who you were yesterday, not to who someone else is today."

In the past, I used to worry that nobody would take my business seriously because I look at least 15 years younger than my actual age. It was only when I realized I was comparing myself to other (older) people that I became less self conscious.

Later, when I started reading Tarot cards professionally, I worried that my business might suffer because I don't dress in flowing kimonos or other stereotypical metaphysical outfits. Once again, I was comparing myself to other people. And I was worried for no reason.

If today was your first day of piano lessons, I sure hope you wouldn't compare yourself to Beethoven. But that's what so many of us do. You see a successful author or musician and assume you suck because you're not further along or on the same level.

When you see other people excelling at what you'd like to do, see it as evidence that it's possible for you too. That's what a rich witch would do.

"It's possible for me too."- Denise Duffield Thomas

DON'T WAIT FOR PERMISSION

"Ask for forgiveness, not permission."- Grace Hopper

In my early days as a mentor, dozens of my students confessed to me that they never felt ready to put themselves out there. I had to tell them that "feeling ready" is a myth. Nobody ever feels ready until AFTER they do the thing they are afraid to do. I've earned thousands and thousands of dollars by putting myself out there before I ever felt ready.

"We're taught at an early age that we're not good enough. That someone else has to choose us in order for us to be…what? Blessed? Rich? Certified? Legitimized? Educated? Partnership material?" — **James Altucher, Choose Yourself**

There's no such thing as "ready"…after a certain number of years, there is no readiness fairy who grants you permission. You have to start NOW, where you are, and only then will you feel ready.

You're ready. I wouldn't lie to you. And even though you don't need it, here's a permission slip from me to you:

PERMISSION SLIP

I give myself permission to
_____.

PART 3: RICH WITCH RITUALS

WHAT IS A RITUAL?

"If theater is a ritual, then dance is too... It's as if the threads connecting us to the rest of the world were washed clean of preconceptions and fears. When you dance, you can enjoy the luxury of being you." —
Paulo Coelho, The Witch of Portobello

There's a lot of confusion about rituals and habits. But there's a big difference between the two. Remember, habits are automatic and often mindless.

Rituals, on the other hand, are done for the sake of doing them. Rituals are more *meaningful* than mindless habits.

The rituals in this section will help you increase your wealth.

CITRINE RITUAL

"Citrine is also known as "success stone" because it brings success and prosperity, especially in business. And it is also called the "Merchant's Stone" because of the practice of placing this stone in the cash registers at stores."- crystalbenefits.com

Ingredients: A piece of citrine. You can get citrine from a crystal shop or buy a piece online. If your crystal feels cold to the touch, that means it's real.

Step One: Hold the citrine in your right hand as you visualize accomplishing your financial goal. Do this for at least 30 seconds. Allow yourself to get excited about spending the money on what it is you desire. See yourself going on that trip or buying that house. Feel the happy feelings!

Step two: Putthe citrine in your wallet next to your money. Everytime you see your money, you'll see the citrine crystal too, which will send energy toward your goals.

Other crystals for increasing prosperity: green aventurine, jade, amethyst

THANK YOUR MONEY

"Money is such an amazing teacher: What you choose to do with your money shows whether you are truly powerful or powerless." Suze Orman

Every time you pay for something, you have a huge opportunity to create more wealth. Say what?! If you are always grateful for having the money to buy the groceries (or whatever it is you're buying), you will always have plenty. Thank your money. Appreciate it. Literally say thank you to it outloud or in your head.

Your attitude when paying determines whether you're grateful or not. Realize that by giving, you are also receiving something in exchange. But if you act stingy, the universe will act stingy with you as well.

A rich witch I know shared this tip with me. She said that by telling her money to come back with friends, she always has cash on hand.

You can say the following to the money in your wallet:

"Money, tell your friends far and wide to come back to me multiplied."

You don't have to say this outloud every time you spend money (or you may get some very weird looks at the store), but you can say it in your mind if you like each time.

MONEY BATH

"There must be quite a few things that a hot bath won't cure, but I don't know many of them." Sylvia Plath

Ingredients: Epsom salt, a red or green candle, your money jar from the previous spell, a chamomile tea bag

Moonphase: any

Step one: Turn on the faucet of your bathtub. Imagine that the water is money filling the tub. (You can even close your eyes and imagine diving into the pile of money like Scrooge Mcduck). Fill the tub with water and throw the chamomile tea bag in. Add a cup of epsom salt to the bathwater.

STEP TWO: SET YOUR MONEY JAR ON THE LEDGE OF THE TUB WHERE YOU CAN SEE IT

STEP THREE: LIGHT THE CANDLE AND PLACE IT ON THE LEDGE OF THE TUB WHERE YOU CAN SEE IT

Step four: Get in the tub and think of what you are requesting the money for. The idea here is to give the money a place to go.

For example: I request this money for taking a trip to London.

Step five: Using your hand, stir the bathwater clockwise three times as you imagine spending the money on your desired outcome.

For example: In the London trip example above, you'd see yourself flying on the airplane, visiting all the London sights, enjoying fish and chips and hearing all the British accents etc.

Step six: Relax and gaze at your money jar for a few minutes. This will charge it with your intentions and impress them in your subconscious mind. Get out of the tub, blow the candle out and dry off.

My client Mikayla was not a fan of baths but she decided to give this spell a whirl anyway because she really wanted to put a down payment on a house. Shortly after casting this spell, she heard about a surfing contest. Mikayla surfed for fun but had never surfed competitively before. She thought of the house she wanted and decided to go for it. She called me ecstatic about winning $10,000 in the surfing contest shortly after.

Another friend of mine used this ritual. She's moving to her dream house in San Diego soon!

Why this works: Water is a powerful conductor of energy and helps to magnify your intentions. You didn't think baths were just for getting clean, did you? With this ritual, you're using the power of water, the power of your intentions, creative visualization AND spellwork for a quadruple whammy!

You can do this ritual as often as once a week if you wish.

Create a Sigil

"Sigils are a means of symbolizing desire and giving it a form that prevents thought on that particular desire… and allows it free passage to the sub-consciousness." – A.O. Spare

A sigil is a powerful symbol that anchors your desired outcome in your subconscious so that you can create this outcome without trying so darn hard. Sigils are a form of Chaos Magic. The bottom line is, they work. Let's get crafty today, shall we?

You don't have to be an artist to create a sigil that works. The power of the sigil will be in your intention. So tell your critical left brain to 'go take a hike' while you create this, okay? Let's go!

Ingredients: a pen or marker or crayon in your favorite color, 2 sheets of white paper (glitter is optional) ☐☐☐

Moonphase: any

Step one: Write out a goal pertaining to your finances in present tense.

Example: "I have recurring passive income that allows me to travel when I want."

Don't just say, "I'm successful." You have to define and literally write out what success means for you.

Step two: Cross out all the vowels in the sentence you wrote in step one. Then rewrite the sentence with just the consonants. It will look like gibberish.

Example from my sentence above: hhv rc rr ng pss v ncm tht llw m t trvl whn wnt

Step three: Cross out any repeating letters and rewrite the remaining letters below.

Example: H v r c n g p s v m t h w

STEP FOUR: DRAW A CIRCLE ON A FRESH SHEET OF WHITE PAPER WITH YOUR FAVORITE COLOR OF PEN/MARKER/CRAYON

STEP FIVE: DRAW EACH LETTER INSIDE THE CIRCLE. BE CREATIVE AND DON'T MAKE THE LETTERS SO OBVIOUS.

STEP SIX: CHARGE YOUR SIGIL WITH ENERGY. REMEMBER THOSE CUTE KITTEN VIDEOS? DO SOMETHING THAT MAKES YOU HAPPY AND FULL OF ENERGY, SUCH AS LAUGHING, DANCING ENERGETICALLY,

HAVING SOME FUN
WITH OR WITHOUT
A PARTNER �� �,
AND THEN STARE
AT THE SIGIL
INTENTLY.

STEP SEVEN: BURY THE SIGIL AND FORGET ABOUT IT.

Sigils may seem simple, but they are so powerful. My clients have used sigils to get higher paying jobs, land new clients, and to receive so much more. I used a sigil to create an extra $2000 recently.

Why it works: Your subconscious mind speaks in pictures. Making a sigil is gets you PAST your pesky, limited conscious mind (with all it's blocks and obstacles) and straight to your always working, always creating subconscious mind.

CARE BOX

"Worry is a prayer for something you don't want to happen."

A care box is also known as a prayer box or a God box. You don't have to be religious to use these boxes and receive great results. One of my atheist clients uses her Care Box to communicate with the universe on a regular basis. Althea credits her care box for helping her sleep well and letting things go. If you have money worries, using a care box may help.

Think of your care box as your own private mailbox to the universe. If something is bothering you and you need help letting it go, write it on a slip of paper and stick it in your Care box. Thank the care box each time. The universe will take care of it. Every time you start to worry about it, remind yourself the universe is taking care of it.

You can use any of the following for your care box:
- A bowl
- A basket
- A shoe box
- A jewelry box (I love the little girls' jewelry boxes with the ballerina inside!)
- A gift bag

You can even make a tiny travel Care box out of an Altoids container.

THE BEGINNING OF YOUR NEW LIFE

So friends, there you have it. Practice the habits in this book until they become second nature. Try out some of the spells and rituals. And let me know about your progress and results!

Book a reading with me here:
https://tinyurl.com/lovezelda

You can reuse this code if you like and you can share it with family and friends. If you have any problem with this discount code applying, just let me know via etsy message and I will adjust the price for you. The link does not expire.

Register for your free book bonuses here:
https://tinyurl.com/zeldamailgifts

Then we can keep in touch as you'll be subscribed to my email newsletter.

If you loved this book, please share it with your friends so we can all do wonderful things with our money. That's how we're going to end the Patriarchy, by being powerful women. Post a photo of yourself reading this book with the hashtag #richwitchbook. If enough people do that, I might cave in and join Instagram :)

Please review this book on Amazon so more women can benefit from reading it.

Other Books in this Series

The Manifesting Experiments, available here: https://www.amazon.com/author/zeldab

In The Manifesting Experiments, Amazon best selling author Zelda Barrons invites you to forget everything you know about the law of attraction. Creating real change doesn't require you to attract anything. Instead, this unconventional guide shows you how to manifest now using the law of assumption (results backed by science).

Forget about getting free cups of coffee, instead, Zelda spills the tea about the law of assumption and shows you how to get whatever you want, including:

Manifest seemingly impossible appearance changes, weight loss and health in yourself AND others
Manifest finding lost objects, people, pets and more
Manifest mystical powers and psychic abilities, telepathy and more
Remove anything and anyone from your life with this hidden power
Manifest love, relationships, friendships, a text from a certain person
Manifest money, success, wealth and fame, no matter what the state of the economy
Change someone else's state for the better
Change your past (Zelda reveals the shamanic technique that guarantees results)

Here's some awesome things my clients have manifested:

Getting someone out of jail
Getting back together with their ex (many, many people have requested this)
Getting married
Winning a national dance competition
Moving to San Francisco
Free concert tickets
A healthy cat
Health for family members
Finding a lost pet
Children's behavior improving (for special needs children)
Money, clients
Social media "fame"
Getting sponsored by a clothing brand

The Rich Witch Guided Manifesting Journal, **available here:**
https://www.amazon.com/author/zeldab

The Rich Witch Guided Manifesting Journal helps you rewire your brain for more fun, funds and love so you can manifest the quick and easy way. To manifest is to bring something into your existence, like reaching a goal. This book requires no tools or ingredients, except your open mind and imagination.

I've taken everything I've learned about the brain, the mind, psychology and universal laws, quantum physics, the law of attraction and the law of assumption and distilled it into some very important questions that you will answer on the following pages in this guided journal to get you FAST results.

You see, your subconscious mind acts like a valve or filter that filters out everything that it deems not important to your survival. So how do we perceive more of the picture? How do you tell your brain what is important to you so you can create what you want now?

By changing your focus and writing it down in a special way you will discover inside. Answer the crucial questions on the pages in this journal and watch your world change like magic right before your eyes.

With this manifesting journal, there is no "wrong" way to use it. If like, you can focus on one goal or desire per page. Or you can repeat (the brain LOVES repetition) and focus on the same desire for multiple pages until it shows up in your world.

Reviews from my readers for my other books:
"There's science, there's practical information, there's inspiration! I found several ideas/theories inspiring, so I am not only read it myself, I ordered 8 more to send to my close friends, someone I care, for them to study and I firmly believe Zelda's book is going to change their road ahead! Zelda is doing a great thing for all of us on this planet, you will regret if you miss it! Go get the book, GOGOGO!"

"This teaches manifestation of the the things we desire, in essence it is the law of attraction. It is a really fun book, full of little stories as examples to guide you on your journey to manifestation. The book is very well written and also easy to understand."

"I love the way Zelda explains how and why it works. I highly recommend this book even if you are already a manifesting queen!"

ABOUT THE AUTHOR

Zelda Barrons lives in a magical world full of possibility. She is a writer, psychic, artist and self-taught Tarot Reader who enjoys exploring the world with her husband.

Get a reading here:
https://www.etsy.com/shop/tarotpsychicoracle

Want even more?

I absolutely love to create. So if you want to see Rich Witch Oracle Cards or a Rich Witch online course, let me know by hopping on the waiting list here: http://tinyurl.com/zeldamailgifts

Resources Mentioned in the Book

Maru Iabichela: infinitereceiving.com

Kim Eibrink Jansen on youtube or kimeibrinkjansen.com

Brad Yates EFT on youtube

The Witch Wound: www.kimberlyjones.com

Made in United States
Cleveland, OH
25 November 2024